Please return/renew this item by the last date shown

worcestershire
countycouncil
Libraries & Learning

Reduce, Reuse, Recycle

Plastic

Alexandra Fix

www.heinemann.co.uk/library

Visit our website to find out more information about **Heinemann Library** books.

To order:

☎ Phone ++44 (0)1865 888066

▤ Send a fax to ++44 (0)1865 314091

💻 Visit the Heinemann Bookshop at www.heinemann.co.uk/library to browse our catalogue and order online.

First published in Great Britain by Heinemann Library, Halley Court, Jordan Hill, Oxford OX2 8EJ, part of Harcourt Education.
Heinemann is a registered trademark of Harcourt Education Ltd.

Editorial: Cassie Mayer and Diyan Leake
Design: Steven Mead and Debbie Oatley
Picture research: Ruth Blair
Production: Duncan Gilbert

Origination: Chroma Graphics (Overseas) Pte Ltd
Printed and bound in China by South China Printing Company Ltd

ISBN 978 0 431 90758 1
12 11 10 09 08

10 9 8 7 6 5 4 3 2

British Library Cataloguing in Publication Data
Fix, Alexandra, 1950-
  Plastic. - (Reduce, reuse, recycle)
  1. Plastic scrap - Juvenile literature 2. Plastic scrap - Recycling - Juvenile literature 3. Waste minimization - Juvenile literature
  I. Title
  363.7'288

Acknowledgements
The publishers would like to thank the following for permission to reproduce photographs: Alamy pp. **4** (Michael Klinec), **5** (Thorsten Indra), **8** (Lourens Smack), **12** (Mike Greenslade), **13** (David Ball), **15** (Manor Photography), **17** (Sébastien Baussais), **19** (Agripicture Images), **20** (Kim Karpeles), **22** (Photofusion Picture Library), **24** (David R. Frazier Photolibrary, Inc.); Corbis pp. **10** (Alberto Esteves/EPA), **14** (Ariel Skelley), **23** (Master Photo Syndecation/SYGMA), **25**, **27** (Bob Krist); Getty Images p. **21** (Digital Vision); Ginny Stroud-Lewis p. **6**; Harcourt Education pp. **16** (Ginny Stroud-Lewis), **26** (Ginny Stroud-Lewis); Harcourt Index p. **7**; Science Photo Library pp. **9** (Philippe Spaila), **11** (George Lepp/Agstock), **18**.

Cover photograph reproduced with permission of Corbis (Randy Faris).

The publishers would like to thank Simon Miller for his assistance in the preparation of this book.

Every effort has been made to contact copyright holders of any material reproduced in this book. Any omissions will be rectified in subsequent printings if notice is given to the publishers.

Contents

Some words are shown in bold, **like this**. You can find out what they mean by looking in the glossary.

What is plastic waste?

These plastic bottles have been saved for recycling.

People use plastic every day. Water bottles, sandwich bags, and food containers are common plastic items. Plastic is strong and can last a long time, but it is not easy to get rid of plastic.

Plastic waste is plastic that is thrown away. When plastic is buried in the ground, it takes many, many years to disappear. Many plastic items can be reused or **recycled**. This would waste less plastic.

If a lot of plastic is thrown away, it can take hundreds of years to **decay**.

What is made of plastic?

Many household items are made of plastic. There are plastic water bottles, milk bottles, bins and bin bags, storage bags, and hangers. Outdoor furniture such as chairs can also be made of plastic.

59%
fat

Baking ✓
Frying ✓
Roasting ✓
Spreading ✓

59%
fat

Baking ✓
Frying ✓
Roasting ✓
Spreading ✓

Many food items are packaged in plastic.

Some parts of racing cars are made of plastic so the cars will be lighter and faster.

Many toys, balls, helmets, and games are made of plastic. Some clothes are made from plastic threads. Carpets, boats, **electronics**, and car parts can be made of plastic, too.

7

Where does plastic come from?

Plastic is made from oil or natural gas found deep in the earth. Oil is mixed with **chemicals** and heated. This mixture becomes soft or liquid plastic.

↑ These plastic pellets will be used to make a plastic item.

Hot liquid plastic is poured into a mould and cooled down to make these toy blocks.

Plastic is made at **factories**. It can be moulded into shapes such as food containers or made into long threads to make larger items.

Will we always have plastic?

Plastic is made from oil.

Oil is the main ingredient in most plastic. Oil is a **non-renewable resource**. If our oil supply gets used up it will be gone forever.

Scientists are starting to use corn and natural sugars to make plastic. These materials are **renewable resources**. They also **decay** faster than plastic made from oil.

Plastic made from corn oil is better for the **environment**.

Index